junkstyle

junkstyle

Melanie Molesworth

photography by
Tom Leighton

RYLAND
PETERS
& SMALL
ON NEW YORK

Designer **Luana Gobbo**
Senior editor **Henrietta Heald**
Production manager **Patricia Harrington**
Editorial director **Julia Charles**
Publishing director **Alison Starling**

Text by **Melanie Molesworth** and
Alice Westgate

First published in the UK in 1998
This compact edition published in 2006 by
Ryland Peters & Small
20–21 Jockey's Fields
London WC1R 4BW

10 9 8 7 6 5 4 3 2

ISBN 978-1-84597-094-9

A CIP record for this book is available
from the British Library.

Printed in China.

contents

introduction

TREASURE HUNTING
this page
*Great sources of
junk style include
second-hand stores,
such as the* brocantes
*found in France, and
country antiques fairs.*

A CLASSIC FIND
left
*A Lloyd Loom-style sofa
fits in anywhere. A fresh
coat of white paint and
a simple milk-coloured
canvas seatcover give
an instant update.*

Demonstrating beyond doubt that one person's junk is someone else's treasure, this book all about doing new, unexpected, stylish things with objects that might otherwise be forgotten or thrown away. It values possessions that have been loved in an earlier life above those that are pristine and soulless, and it shows that cracks, chips and blemishes can be part of an item's attraction and proof of its uniqueness.

Although the word 'junk' may describe anything that has been discarded, some so-called rubbish is too good to be consigned to a skip. Many pieces cry out to be recycled and reintegrated into our homes. Discerning devotees of junk style pick these pieces from among the clutter, upgrade them and incorporate their timeless qualities into their lives. The photographs in this book depict real homes filled with all manner of recycled pieces that are unfailingly chic and elegant. Their owners have embraced the idea of junk style with such wholehearted enthusiasm that they spend most of their weekends looking for more examples of faded beauty. For these people, using junk has become a way of life. Indeed, much of the appeal of this look is that you cannot simply go and purchase it off the shelf. The hunt itself usually constitutes half the fun. Flea markets, antiques fairs, car-boot sales, architectural salvage yards, home and office clearances, auctions, charity outlets and second-hand shops are among the excellent sources of potential discoveries ranging from the everyday to the exceptional. Each source of junk style is unpredictable

GOLD AND DROSS
this page
*Never forget that there
is a fine balance to be
struck between being
the first to pick a bargain
and being the fool who
goes home with a dud.*

SPOTTING POTENTIAL
opposite
*Before buying any piece
for your home, consider
where you might put it.
Think beyond traditional
uses – for example, a
galvanized bucket could
contain firewood.*

and offers up its own secrets: the acquisitions you end up
with depend on where you look, the time of your arrival and
what your personal tastes are.

You do not need the skills of a knowledgeable antiques
dealer to pick up bargains. The secret is to look for features
that particularly appeal to you – a texture, a subtly aged
colour, skilful craftsmanship, a decorative flourish or an
object's practicality – and to make a purchase based on
aesthetic values rather than on price tag or provenance.
Salvaged items sourced with care, restored with love and
introduced to your home with flair will always be its most
interesting and expressive pieces.

Don't be afraid to put a contemporary spin on whatever
you find, combining old with new in a way that reflects your
own personal style. Happy hunting!

inspirational
FINDS

colour

The most successful foil for junk style is undoubtedly white or cream. The sheer simplicity of white and its clean, timeless look provide the perfect contemporary background for any type of junk furniture, from polished dark wooden tables to classic 1950s sofas in jazzily coloured loose covers.

A judicious injection of strong colour as an accent on paintwork can add vibrancy to an otherwise cool scheme. But choosing the right shade is vital. Harsh tones can overpower the

WARM EFFECT right
Yellow and cream walls provide a sympathetic backdrop to distinctively shaped furniture finds.

HIGHLIGHTS far right
A single strong colour on the ceiling and the window frame gives this room an edge.

subtlety of natural materials and dominate organic pigments that have been gradually dulled by the bleaching effect of the sun and a lifetime of wear and tear. Muted shades that mimic the natural effects of ageing, such as pale pastels or earthy terracotta tones, can offer the best complement.

MUTED SHADES right

A colour scheme can dictate the mood of a room. The calm, restful atmosphere of this old Long Island barn is enhanced by the subtle shades chosen for the paint on the walls and the simple furniture.

METALLICS left

A Paris apartment has been brought up to date with a coat of white paint and an eclectic mixture of metal furniture. The lime-effect finish on the old wooden beams and floorboards harmonizes with the chalky patina of weathered metal.

HOT HUES right
Bright jazzy colours were the epitome of 1950s style. Here, classic Robin Day chairs in burnt orange are teamed with other 1950s furniture.

SNAZZY STORAGE
left and below
Imaginative use of paint turns simple cupboard doors into distinctive decorative features.

surfaces

Surfaces that have clearly been touched by the gentle process of ageing are inherited rather than bought – which is why the imperfections typical of junk furniture and other salvaged items are so precious.

Peeling wallpaper, roughly plastered walls, exposed bricks, flaking paint on a door, a rusty headboard, some worn-out rugs, a bare wooden tabletop, flagstones polished by centuries of footsteps – all these elements should be cherished because many years of use have made them the way they are today.

In recognition of the value inherent in age, crumbling walls can be left undecorated, the cracked or dusty bare plaster characterizing the setting in which you can display your treasured junk-shop finds. When it comes to flooring, simplicity is the best approach. Bare boards, sanded down and then either polished with beeswax or limed for a paler, more contemporary look, are an economical and practical option for virtually every room.

PEELING PAPER above
A hallway with remnants of 1950s wallpaper frames a casual still-life of garden paraphernalia.

THE ROUGH WITH THE SMOOTH opposite
Cracked tiles make a practical floor; a rough wall with a road sign brings the outside in; old floorboards are updated; peeling paint creates an inimitable effect.

Explore architectural salvage yards for discarded flagstones and tiles – and reclaim them. Ceramic tiles bought in small batches might not be enough to cover a whole floor, but they can be incorporated into larger-scale designs, or used to create a fire-surround or make a splashback above a sink. Cracked or incomplete tiles are useful, too; they can be broken up and laid down to tessellate an area of floor for the ultimate in waste not, want not.

On walls, layers of old wallpaper and paint can be partially scraped back to reveal the décor chosen by generations of previous occupants. Alternatively, you might chance upon some unopened rolls of old wallpaper – in a house clearance, for example – and decide to use these to conjure up the style of another era.

TEXTURAL MÉLANGE
right
This bedroom wall has been left unrenovated, so that the overall look is a collage of textures.

PATTERN ON PATTERN
far right
Flaking 19th-century wallpaper clings to the walls alongside layers of old paint and plaster.

furniture

Whether you are looking for things that are handsome or quirky, decorative or functional, antique or contemporary, industrial or domestic – or a mixture of many styles – the joy of junk furniture is that there is something somewhere to appeal to everyone. And a house full of junk furniture has a timeless feel, so scour sales, antique shops, and flea markets for pieces that fit in with your home's unique character.

As you become accustomed to shopping in this sort of environment – where a beautiful cabinet might be found hiding beneath a pile of old tea chests – you will grow increasingly adept at distinguishing the interesting and special from the dull and mundane.

SIXTIES STYLE
opposite, left
*This metal swivel chair
was purchased for a
song at an Amsterdam
office warehouse.*

GEOMETRIC LINES
opposite, right
*The distinctively angular
lines of a classic Robin
Day armchair create a
sharp, boxy shape.*

OUTSIDE IN
this page
*A weathered garden
bench was chosen for its
simple curved lines and
crusted-paint surface.*

PLEASE BE SEATED
left and below
*Raffia chairs are placed
to take advantage of the
sea view; a folding chair
serves as a garden table.*

ALL TYPES opposite,
clockwise from top left
*An American rocker rests
on a beachhouse deck;
a slatted French folding
chair makes a spare seat
for an impromptu guest;
a well-worn chair waits
outside a New York thrift
shop for a loving buyer;
fancy metal seats are
displayed for sale in a
junk lovers' paradise.*

chairs

Junk shops and flea markets are usually filled with chairs that have stood the test of time. Whether your heart's desire is an assortment of seating for a dining room, a dressing-table stool, some metal garden furniture or a cosy armchair, you are almost certain to strike it lucky. Try each piece for size before you buy, and look for indications that the chair has been comfortable enough to have been well used in the past – the sagging seat of an armchair or a wooden armrest that shines from years of use are both good signs.

If the basic character of the piece is right, quick and easy alterations such as adding a new cover, a simple fabric throw or some plump cushions will hide any major faults.

SLATTED STYLE
this page
A casual arrangement of furniture borrowed from the garden looks surprisingly elegant in an Amsterdam loft.

PARK CHAIRS
opposite, left and right
Metal-framed wooden chairs such as these, on show at an antiques fair, can make a stylish set of dining chairs.

It is rare to come across a complete set of matching dining chairs or kitchen chairs in a junk shop, so – rather than search in vain – consider buying an assortment of single chairs individually, as and when you see them, and gradually build up an idiosyncratic selection of your own.

Look for examples that have arms and gently sloping high backs for ultimate comfort as you dine, and make tie-on seat cushions from scraps of fabric to soften their look as well as their feel. You will probably find that your guests are so comfortable that they will want to linger around the table for a long time after the meal is over.

Wicker tub chairs and metal garden chairs – especially folding slatted ones that can be stored flat and then pressed into service if you have unexpected guests – are all worth considering, along with more conventional ladderbacks and carvers. Old wooden chairs that were once used in church halls or school rooms often crop up in junk shops alongside

SOLIDITY left
Some chairs, such as this chunky, box-seated example, are so sturdily constructed that they clearly have years of useful life left in them.

VERSATILITY below left
Placed at convenient points, chairs can make useful extra surfaces.

ELEGANCE right
This pale wooden chair is placed in such a way as to show off its glowing colour and fine curves.

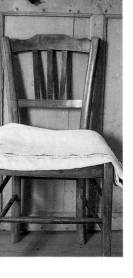

tall laboratory stools and rush-seated café chairs. All are perfect for kitchen seating since they are particularly sturdy and often stackable – an asset if you are short of space.

Elegant one-off buys such as rockers and woven Lloyd Loom chairs will be quite at home in either a bedroom or bathroom, creating a quiet corner in which to relax.

For work spaces, office clearances are a good source of seating. Adjustable architects' chairs and leather-covered swivel chairs are extremely practical as well as being better-looking than modern options. Make sure that you buy an office chair that is the correct height for use with your desk so you will be able to work in comfort as well as style.

CHARACTER inset
You may fall in love with some chairs on account of a detail such as a studded leather seat.

KITSCH main picture
An 1950s chair is the focal point in a corner of this otherwise sparsely decorated apartment.

benches
and sofas

A new sofa is expensive, so a junk-shop alternative, even if it needs a few repairs, can be an exceptional bargain. Metal-framed daybeds, benches and chaises longues are also much sought-after because they are sociable pieces of furniture that give a room a relaxed and casual air, especially when strewn with an inviting assortment of cushions or covered with an old rug or kilim.

A generous seating arrangement is a must in a living room – but is also wonderful in the sort of kitchen that is the hub of family life, a quiet bedroom where you might retreat with a book, a corner of a roomy bathroom, or as a much-needed place of rest in a study.

Whichever part of the house a sofa is destined for, comfort should be top priority when you are searching for the best buys. Sprawl out on a sofa before

SACKCLOTH left
Old French flour sacks have been used to make cushion covers for a pretty bench. The covers are designed in such a way as to set off the stitched strip and logo.

REINVENTING THE WHEEL above
An old cartwheel, which was rescued at a sale of redundant farming implements, becomes a work of art when placed in an interior setting.

you make a decision to ensure that it is as comfortable as it is good-looking. To find out whether wooden, wicker and metal-framed benches meet the same criteria, buy and fit some feather-filled squabs. The bench can then be used as overflow seating in the sitting room or space-saving seating alongside a rectangular dining table – perfect for children to use at family meals.

Leather-covered sofas age beautifully and are lucky flea-market finds that may need only the odd patch here and there to make them serviceable. Along with classic Knoles and Chesterfields, they are the ultimate in shabby chic.

To hide leaking stuffing or a fitted cover that is too tatty to leave on show, make some loose covers from a fabric that complements the sofa's faded look, or shroud the whole thing in a large swathe of cloth; ignore the folds and creases and simply tuck in the edges. Look for faded curtains, old sackcloth, shawls and bedspreads with a lived-in look, and your 'new' upholstery will not detract from the sofa's dated charm.

COVER STORY left

Sturdy cream linen sheets help to protect a generous sofa from the rigours of family life in this Dutch living room.

CREASED UP above

Provided its framework is sound, any old sofa can be given a new lease of life with a simple cream canvas cover.

tables

From old cable reels to large trunks, there are numerous junk and flea-market finds that can be transformed into tables. Add a scrubbed plank bench, a simple trestle and a delicate wirework console and you'll realize that junk is a potential source of every surface you'll ever need, from dining tables and bedside cabinets to makeshift desks.

For kitchens, it's hard to beat old pine refectory tables, which are easy to find in all shapes and sizes. They are very practical and, given a coat or two of tough varnish, can put up with the onslaught of hot pans. Choose the biggest refectory table your kitchen can take, since it will probably be used for paperwork, hobbies and reading the newspaper as well as for dining and food preparation.

A better solution than a refectory table in a limited space is a drop-leaf table, which can accommodate a larger gathering of people when necessary, while tables with drawers are useful for additional storage. Small steel-topped tables and butcher's blocks can provide extra work surfaces when space is at a premium.

Even if your kitchen is on the small side, keep a lookout for an elegant marble-topped café table with cast-iron legs or a wicker side table that will fit snugly into a corner and enable two people to eat there comfortably.

A small table in the hallway is useful as a surface for keys and mail or as a place to put a lamp or display a vase of fresh flowers for an instant welcome.

BRIGHT WHITE
opposite
White unifies an eclectic mix of junk furniture for a 1990s look. The fluted table legs contrast with the cool swivel chairs.

SWEET DREAMS
above
An old garden table with twisted metal legs works just as well beside a bed as it did surrounded by chairs on a veranda.

Look for an unusual piece of furniture to make a striking first impression: for example, a sewing-machine bench, an ornate metal-framed table with a glass top or a decorative wooden console will establish the junk-style look as soon as you step inside the front door.

Occasional tables are indispensable in a living room as surfaces for books, magazines or tea trays, for example, so search junk shops and scour garage sales for anything from small wooden stools and folding butler's tray tables to wooden tea trolleys and stacking coffee tables.

Many of these options can also be useful in bedrooms in preference to conventional matching cabinets on each side of a bed, or in bathrooms, where they can be piled with fresh linens or baskets of soaps.

If you find a table at a flea market that really is past its best for interior use but still has appealing features, there is a good chance that it will come in handy in the potting shed or garden as a workbench or plant stand.

RECYCLING
this page
A huge cable wheel becomes a fashion designer's work table in a Paris apartment.

PEDAL POWER
opposite, above
A sewing-machine stand complete with foot pedal makes an unusual side table in a rustic space.

STARS AND STRIPES
opposite, below
National pride obviously dictated the decoration for this brightly painted, two-tier table.

fabrics

Many junk shops are full of textiles such as curtains, bed linens, blankets, quilts, lace, mattress tickings – and even fabric remnants of all sizes in innumerable colours, weights, textures and patterns. The inimitable look and feel of faded chintz, old velvet, time-softened linens and kitsch prints will make an interior feel snug and lived in, so include a variety of these fabrics in your junk-style room designs, mixing them with modern pieces if you like.

Use more precious pieces sparingly in a position where they can take pride of place, and allow less expensive ones to hang in generous folds. Vintage fabrics can be patched or left threadbare and unironed to imbue your surroundings with an air of relaxed living.

TICKING OVER left
There is a huge range of traditional mattress tickings available; various stripes and colours often work well together.

PIANO COVER right
A pretty striped cotton in French blue contrasts with blue checks on the chair and helps to hide a piano in this small room.

LADDER OF SUCCESS above
An old ladder simply propped up against a wall makes an original towel rail, useful in the bathroom or the kitchen.

A TOUCH OF LACE
below
*Recycled curtains
provide a delicate lacy
undersheet beneath
the top cover.*

RAMBLING ROSES
below right
*A rose-patterned curtain
spread over a dormitory
bed transforms the
mood of the room.*

Vintage fabrics have a charm that cannot be replicated by modern materials, however faithful fabric companies may be at reproducing old designs. The fabrics that survive years of good service relatively intact tend to be the durable ones. They are usually made from natural rather than man-made fibres, and they complement the other natural textures, such as wood, that form such an important element of junk style.

The authentic feel of antique linen or lace, or soft woollen blankets that have been washed so many times the nap has worn smooth, more than compensates for a frayed edge or an occasional hole. Paisleys, florals, stripes, and checks are a useful way to bring a splash of pattern to otherwise subtly

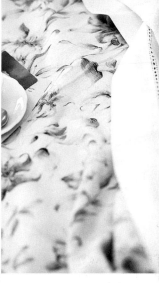

VIOLETS above

Subtle florals, such as this 1950s design, can soften an otherwise coolly decorated room.

FLORAL CHARM above left

A country junk shop's rummage basket was the source of this pretty bedcover, once a curtain.

decorated rooms. Even the most overblown chintz will look charming rather than overpowering when surrounded by the casual restraint of junk style. So drape dining tables with layers of linen and lace for a touch of faded grandeur, dress beds with antique linens, soft counterpanes and feather-filled bolsters, cover sofas and chairs with fabrics such as

PURE WHITE
left and below

*All-white bed linen lends
a monastic feel to a
bedroom. If you need
extra warmth, follow the
example of the owner
of this 19th-century
travelling bed and add
woollen blankets.*

PICNIC CHECKS
right

*Faded blankets in
contrasting pastels were
used to re-upholster this
pair of classic armchairs
with rounded arms; they
are soft, comfortable
oases in a minimally
furnished London loft.*

sensual silk, knobbly chenille, starched
cotton and warm wool to enhance their
comfortable appeal.

To complement rich vintage textiles,
buy new lengths of timeless gingham,
striped ticking, muslin or canvas, and
make them up into loose covers or sew
them into borders. These utility fabrics
blend well with older, more decorative
examples. Try mixing new gingham with
a faded floral, a pristine ticking with
some old checks, an unbleached cotton
with an elegant damask, or a length of
linen with a panel of antique lace.

If you are a diehard recycler, you will
do what generations have done before
you and collect any leftover scraps to
make into a patchwork quilt.

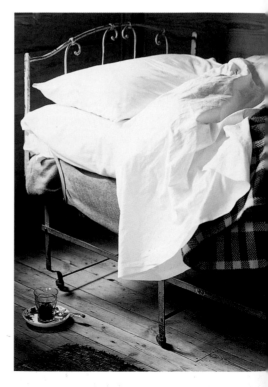

containers
and storage

For innovative storage solutions, junk shops make wonderful hunting grounds. Items ranging from boxes and baskets to cabinets and shelving are essential ingredients of any well-organized home, whether you like to keep a minimalist, clean and contemporary look or to fill your home with a wonderful array of treasured clutter. Search for both conventional and unusual pieces to house your possessions. Useful finds include enamel tins and bread bins, wooden crates, medicine chests, baker's racks, butcher's hooks and an assortment of basketware.

POTS OF STYLE left
Kitchen scales and salt pots sit among storage jars in a monochrome collection from a French country kitchen.

BOXED IN top
A abundance of dents and a rusty, peeling-paint finish simply enhance the charm of these old storage tins.

GREAT CRATES above
These baskets and wine crates, complete with their original lettering, make a relatively cheap but chic storage solution.

small storage

Before the days of mass production and man-made materials, everything from vegetables to soap powder was sold in tins, trays, bags, crates, racks, barrels, boxes and baskets that were carefully packaged and frequently labelled with beautiful lettering to advertise their contents and the producer's identity. The containers were made so durable that many survive today, often cropping up among the junk at stalls and markets after years of being shut away in attics and cellars. All deserve to be given a new lease of life, so buy them to use for storage all around the home. They are far more desirable than the crude replica tins and baskets that are now on the market in response to a revived interest in period pieces.

Wooden grocer's trays and vegetable crates can be used for displaying plants in a conservatory, storing toys in a playroom, growing herbs on a kitchen windowsill or holding supplies of dried goods in the kitchen. Brightly painted

EGG BOX above
A metal box originally used to store eggs has found a new use as a receptacle for letters and paperwork.

ENAMELWARE right
Popular in the 1930s, enamel kitchenware, including bowls, tureens and colanders, is still going strong today.

logos, especially ones that reveal an exotic past, are most sought after. Old shopping bags, picnic hampers and bicycle panniers are covetable for their intricate workmanship as well as their versatility. Fill them with shoes to store under the bed or line them with fabric and use them for laundry.

Enamel tins often appear among kitchenalia in junk stores – sometimes labelled 'flour' or 'sugar', sometimes striped or with coloured lids. French markets offer similar items for storing '*farine*' and '*sucre*' – particularly sought after for recreating rural Provençal style or faded Parisian chic. A mismatched assortment can look wonderful on a kitchen shelf and are just as useful today as they were originally.

Metal trunks, old suitcases and leather collar and hat boxes can be filled with clothes, book and papers before being piled on top of a wardrobe or under a dressing table to create an attractive display as well as making the most of a limited space and reviving age-old household practice. For bathrooms, search for wooden drying racks, linen presses and laundry baskets to store towels, and small shelving units, glass bottles and small baskets for toiletries. Plan chests, bookcases of all shapes and sizes and wooden crates are ideal for books and magazines; they can also be used to hold the accumulations of modern life that add clutter to the clean lines of the junk-style look, while a metal filing cabinet will swallow up household papers, bills and

WELL DRESSED
above left
A utilitarian metal rail is a perfect makeshift wardrobe, allowing a fine array of second-hand clothes to be placed permanently on show.

INVENTIVE IDEAS
from left to right
A row of wooden bird houses crowns a set of painted drawers; the empty spaces where drawers are missing are used to display favourite objects. Barrels, wicker baskets and bowls can be recycled to store everything from fresh laundry to fresh garden produce. A collection of books and glassware is displayed enticingly on open shelves.

GARDEN DISPLAY
above
A rickety wooden stand, originally from a baker's shop, is an attractive addition to this sheltered corner of a garden. It is a convenient place to keep tools and equipment and to display freshly picked fruit and vegetables.

documents. Glass-fronted cabinets and open shelves are useful all around the house. Look out for shop fittings such as drapers' display counters with glass-fronted drawers for original storage units; in the bedroom a single free-standing metal clothes rail can look stylish. Blanket boxes and old leather suitcases also provide capacious storage.

In awkward spaces such as halls try pegs, hat stands, drawstring shoe bags and metal shelving. Panelled wooden doors, in plentiful supply at flea markets, can be fixed over existing alcoves and recesses to make extra cupboards that look as if they have been there for years. Equip them with shelves or rows of hooks and you will have the ideal place to store linen, coats and household equipment.

SAFE AS HOUSES
right
An old-fashioned meat safe is a stylish way to expand kitchen storage.

HERB GARDEN
below
For an instant kitchen garden, drill holes in the base of a wooden crate and plant it with a variety of culinary herbs.

PORTABLE
below left
A shallow-sided crate can be used as an impromptu tray.

cupboards

With a little imagination, the cupboards on sale at flea markets and auctions can provide ingenious storage solutions. For example, an old pie safe would make a good place to store crockery, a pine wardrobe could become a pantry, and a wooden cabinet could find a new role in a bathroom.

Generously proportioned cupboards are at a premium in junk shops because they are such practical and handsome additions to the home, especially in the bedroom, where a freestanding, French-style armoire or a rough-and-ready pine

CUPBOARD LOVE
this page
Painted wall cupboards, simple and ornate, can be found in all shapes and sizes at flea markets.

wardrobe can be stylish. Corner cabinets allow you to make the most of awkward space that would otherwise be wasted. Details such as carving, decorative moulding, coloured-glass insets, a mirrored front panel and attractive door furniture all make a purchase worthwhile.

Easier to carry back from your junk-shop forays are smaller cupboards, useful for storage throughout the home. Glass-fronted cabinets are ideal if you are happy to put what's inside the cupboard on show. Whether it is tins of baked beans or your best crockery, arrange the contents attractively.

Revamping your cupboards with new or reclaimed door knobs, pull handles and decorative and unusual brass or iron hinges, or even just polishing up the existing ones with steel wool, can work wonders, as can replacing cracked or warped door panels with etched or clear glass, chicken wire or a length of fabric gathered on a wire.

lamps
and lighting

Lighting has an enormous impact on the way we feel about a room and the way we see the objects that fill it. Even the no-frills approach of a simply shaded bulb or a naked candle flame has a profound effect on a room's atmosphere. So, when you are creating a specific look from your junk-shop finds, don't ignore details such as lighting.

While there is no need to keep strictly to one style or period, you should strive to be sympathetic to the overall look – and be aware that many modern light fittings could look horribly out of place. Instead, install decorative light fittings acquired from your favourite stalls and markets, and they will add to the overall character of junk style.

RISE AND FALL this page
This elegant, adjustable pendant light proves that you don't have to choose a modern fitting for versatility.

LIGHTS FANTASTIC
this page, clockwise
from left

*Search flea markets for
period light fittings such
as a decorative wirework
candleholder, a French
glass shade to hang over
a table or a clip-on metal
spot lamp that is perfect
for kitchen task lighting.*

Salvage yards and second-hand outlets are usually well stocked with original light fittings ripped out of old houses in the name of modernization. Many such items are still functional and, if rescued and reused, can last another lifetime. Second-hand electric-light fittings should always be checked and installed by a qualified electrician, so that any worn or damaged wiring or connections can be replaced. Once their safety has been certified, old fittings can do a more stylish job than their modern equivalents, which are often too high-tech to combine easily with more traditional junk elements.

Candlelight creates a warmth and romance that fits in perfectly with the relaxed nature of junk style, so use it as much as possible. Candle-holders come in many different forms, from containers designed for that purpose to former jam jars. For a decorative flourish, old pewter candlesticks, perhaps dented or worn smooth by years of polishing, can be picked up relatively cheaply from among grander antiques. More rustic options include metal hurricane lamps and storm lanterns, which look great on a mantelpiece or table, but which are also useful outside on summer evenings.

A GOOD SIGN left
As well as buying old lights, you can adapt other junk items to camouflage modern light fittings. French lighting designer Alexis Aufray made this highly original light fitting out of an old rusted-metal road sign. The bulb behind floods the wall with light.

Before you set off on your first foraging expedition, plan the lighting scheme for your entire home, deciding what style of fittings you need and where they will go. Each room should have something to provide general or ambient lighting – a central pendant, for example. There should also be individual task lights over desks, beside armchairs and in kitchens to facilitate studying, reading or cooking. Finally, you will need

STORM FRONT above
Whether used to light an alfresco meal or simply as outdoor decoration, hurricane lamps are romantic and stylish.

CANDLE LIGHT above
Bulbous storm lanterns are suspended from a beam on wire hangers.

ON THE ROAD right
A roadworker's lamp finds a new use in an Avignon restaurant.

GASLIGHT far right
A mirror reflects the metal wick control of an old gas-light fitting with its original glass lantern.

some sort of accent lighting to draw the eye towards particular items that you wish to highlight, such as a work of art or an attractive collection of objects on display. Lighting to fulfil all these roles – plus any pieces you fall in love with on the spot for their purely decorative qualities and elect to find a place for as soon as you return home – can easily be found in junk shops.

Finding a coloured or plain glass-drop chandelier might well be one of the highlights of your search – with a bit of cleaning and perhaps a replacement

glass drop here and there, it will give off a delicate twinkling light that is grand but never gaudy. Hang it in conventional style over a dining table or somewhere more unusual, such as a bathroom, to give an air of opulence.

Alternatively, you can decide to use a chandelier purely as a beautifully decorative object and not have it wired to the electricity supply for use as a light. If you go for this option, hang the chandelier near a source of natural light such as window so the glass drops catch and reflect the sunlight.

TAKE THE FLOOR
left

The ornately designed floor lamp beside the open fireplace makes this an ideal place to relax with a good book. A model dog provides suitably silent company.

Candelabra can make similarly grand statements, but remember that lit candles should never be left unattended, and the smoke can leave stains on a plain white ceiling.

Look out, too, for glass or ceramic uplighters that will wash an entire wall with gentle light, and for elegant standard lamps, with or without their original shades. Pleated shades to fit – silk if you are lucky, paper if you are not – can often be found separately, along with an assortment of other shades in glass, metal, parchment, wicker or fabric. These can either be paired off with other lamp bases you might find or easily adapted to use with pendant fittings. Wall sconces – some incorporating candle-holders, others fitted with kitsch, flame-shaped bulbs – are also much sought after, especially wrought-iron models in ornate floral or foliage designs. The best finds are always the classic designs – in this case, old adjustable anglepoise desk lamps, tall metal standard lamps with extending arms and traditional brass picture lights.

A GOOD ANGLE
above

Anglepoise lamps are essential accessories in traditional or modern offices. Their flexible and stylish design has altered little over the years.

CLEAR YOUR DESK
above left

Garage sales are a good source of adjustable desk lamps. Check that the springs are sound before you buy. If they are too tight, the arms will not budge; if too loose, your lamp will flop.

glass, china
and ceramics

The delicate floral china plates and cut-glass vases that were cherished by our grandmothers are now fashionable again and are an integral part of junk style. Think of a jug filled with flowers, a china bowl planted with hyacinths, a shelf laden with dishes, a dresser piled high with earthenware, or a table set with an assortment of china. Reasonable prices make it easy to build up a collection for everyday use or for decoration. Riffling through piles of plates, searching for an unusual design, and imagining how a glass bottle would look when cleaned, adds to the enjoyment.

MIX AND MATCH left
Collect assorted pieces of cheap glassware and cutlery for everyday use.

SOMETHING SPECIAL above left
Glass vases, dishes and cake plates are useful one-off purchases.

DECORATION right
Intricately patterned spoons, some tied in a bundle with blue wool, make a pretty still-life on a glass dish. Although the items do not match, their styles are similar enough to result in a harmonious whole.

Gone are the days when we had to have a fully matching dinner service. Now, table settings with character can comprise mismatched plates, odd glasses and an assortment of cutlery. Whether you are hosting a dinner party or simply having a few friends around for coffee, a casual mix of glass and china will make it an easy-going affair.

Tableware makes up only a fraction of the pieces you are likely to come across. If you spot a bowl and jug set, a dish or some dressing-table china, your junk-shop discoveries could also be used to adorn your bathroom and bedroom. Similarly, bottles and jars that were discarded years ago when the milk, medicine or ginger beer ran out

SHELF LIFE opposite
Simple wooden shelving is the perfect place to display china plates amassed over 25 years.

SOMETHING FISHY above left
This collection of china is united by a seaside theme, making it witty as well as pretty.

ALL SET above
Among more ordinary china you may be lucky enough to come across a complete dinner set.

USER FRIENDLY below
Flea-market finds are not only for show. If you use them for daily meals, you will come to appreciate them to the full.

often find their way back into the home by means of car-boot sales and house clearances. Use them to display a single stem or lined up en masse on a windowsill. Coloured glass looks particularly good when it filters shafts of sunlight beside a window, so search for old bottles in vivid shades of cobalt blue, soft aqua, deep green or glowing amber. Embossed lettering and original labels, plus lids, stoppers and corks, add to their charm.

IN BLOOM left
Antiques and flowers are combined at the Long Island florists Potted Gardens.

KEEP IT SIMPLE
opposite, clockwise from top left
Plain glassware often makes a perfect vessel for a floral arrangement; you can display single stems in clear tumblers, for example. An antique cachepot has become home to a simple display of hedgerow flowers. A row of inexpensive salt shakers makes an unpretentious and eye-catching display on a shelf in a seaside home. Big containers are ideal for large flowers; this narrow-necked demi-john supports a huge allium.

COCKTAIL KITSCH
top
Plastic glamour-girl swizzle-sticks from the 1950s make a perfect match for these modern classic tumblers.

ROSY OUTLOOK
right
For impromptu displays all over the house, fill cut-glass drinking vessels with seasonal flowers.

collections
and collectables

Any discovery can provide the starting point for a collection of junk objects – from an array of old tobacco tins to a handful of old lead fishing weights. Once you have found something you covet, every subsequent visit to a junk shop will have more momentum because it might reveal just the thing you have been looking for.

A collection speaks volumes about the person who has amassed it, and quirky and highly idiosyncratic items often become the most obsessively sought after. The hunt for picture books, pearl buttons, board games, egg whisks, hats or bird cages can become all-consuming and, when displayed around the house in a decorative way, these objects introduce lovely witty touches.

ARTFUL left and above
The contents of artist Yuri Kuper's former barn in Normandy reveal his fondness for architectural prints as well as various quirky objects such as lock barrels – cherished for their aesthetic rather than monetary value.

BESIDE THE SEA above right
This collection of fishing weights turned up in a local charity shop.

TINWARE left

These battered tins are on show in Yuri Kuper's loft home in New York.

GARDEN SHED below

Collectors' items may be lying forgotten; search out bell jars, flower pots and watering-can roses.

HANDIWORK right

Tools become decorative items in their own right when hung on a wall.

FLAT OUT far right

Choose one type of item – such as an antique flat iron – and look for more wherever you go.

Many other everyday objects are worth collecting – and can often be picked up easily at car-boot sales. The perennial favourite is old kitchenware; some covetable household utensils, such as kettles and weighing scales, can earn their keep as well as enlarge a collection if they are still in working order. Garden tools are also much sought after, especially old cloches, terracotta pots and trugs, which can either adorn a conservatory or be pressed back into service. But not everyone who spends hours searching for the perfect piece to augment their collection ends up with a house full of clutter. Collecting can be compatible with a desire for a more minimal interior. Whatever look you want to create, be precise: discretion and theming are the keys to making discerning purchases from the myriad junk items on offer.

A CUT ABOVE left
Show off your cherished treasures behind glass. Dressmakers' tools and bright napkins go on display in two fine jars.

IN STITCHES right
A still-life is created from a collection of old sewing paraphernalia – much still in its original delightful packaging.

WELL SPUN left
The natural hues of these old silk threads, some still threaded on factory-sized spools, form another collection based on haberdashery.

decoration
and display

Finding ways to arrange the items you have collected from junk shops and flea markets is enormously enjoyable. The more innovative and creative your displays the better, since they will invite you to look at old objects in a new light as well as allowing you to decorate your home with an interesting and personal touch. For small-scale arrangements, corner cupboards, narrow shelves, small cubby holes and old wooden printer's boxes are tailor-made. Displays of belongings make a room feel lived in, so keep them fresh by changing them whenever the mood takes you – or when a buying trip forces you to move things to make room for another unmissable treasure.

ULTRA MARINE
above left
Flying birds, a wooden sailing boat and some spades comprise a distinctly nautical display in a seaside home.

HAT STAND left
An old fruit-picking ladder is used to display a collection of hats in painter Charlotte Culot's Provençal home.

STILL LIFE right
Dried seed heads, ceramics, pictures and shells are the simple ingredients that bring a shelf to life.

HOLY ORDER above

Religious icons fill a shrine-like wooden cupboard in a home in Amsterdam.

THREE IN A ROW right

Simple wooden spades are propped up against the wood-panel wall of a beach house

BEACH FINDS far right

Treasures retrieved from the seashore have been used to cover a selection of small boxes.

JAGGED above right

A rusty saw embellished with wonderful lettering has been given pride of place on a white wall.

Look out for glazed box frames and glass-fronted cabinets in which to show off tiny trinkets. Especially in the kitchen, bigger items can be hung from ceiling racks and wooden airers. Some successful displays arrange like with like so their similarities can be properly grasped. Imagine the effect of seeing a row of identical clear-glass apothecary jars on a bathroom cabinet, or a shelf of spongeware jugs. Other displays work well because of the juxtaposition of different styles, colours and textures: you might love the contrast between contemporary ceramics and old porcelain, or between kitsch artificial flowers and brass candlesticks.

GALLERY overleaf
Treasures varying from a life buoy to a battered shoe last can be used for decoration.

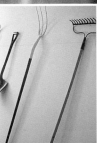

found
objects

Junk-style addicts keep their eyes open
for objects of interest wherever they
go. Whether you are spending a lazy
day on a beach, digging in the garden
or out on a woodland walk, you may
discover a natural wonder or some
man-made object discarded long ago
that can become a treasure in its own
right. Such things are particularly
satisfying to collect since they are close
at hand, easy to find and – best of all –
absolutely free.

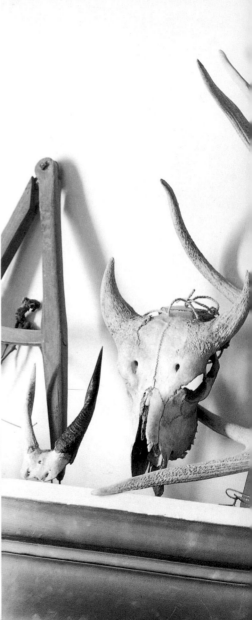

MANTELPIECE
this picture
*These skulls were found
in the Camargue and in
Africa, while the antlers
are from Provence.*

NATURAL SELECTION
left
*A walk in the woods can
yield a wealth of natural
finds, from feathers to
textural stones.*

WOOD AND STONE
far left
*Interesting pieces of
driftwood, wooden bowls
and undressed stone
surfaces give a natural
look in a bathroom.*

IN FULL BLOOM right
An old wooden barrow, complete with its original wheel, has been planted to create an unusual container garden.

IN THE FRAME
this picture
Odd items of cutlery find a new home mounted on white cardboard and put in second-hand frames.

HIDDEN POTENTIAL
far right
Another wheelbarrow languishes in an outhouse awaiting a similar transformation.

Beachcombing is as much fun for adults recapturing childhood memories as it is for children discovering the joys of the seaside for the first time. Scan the high-water mark and you might find jewel-like pieces of sea-smoothed glass washed up alongside delicate feathers, gnarled and twisted lengths of sculptural driftwood, chunks of flint, and maybe a fisherman's basket or float.

As they turn over the soil, gardeners are accustomed to unearthing a wealth of interesting objects. Fragments of pottery, perhaps a section of glazed tile, a cup handle or a section of clay pipe, are all worth keeping. Elsewhere in the garden, old flower pots and wrought-iron brackets are waiting to be discovered and appreciated. Luckier finds are discarded garden tools, such as old rusted rakes and spades, or even an old wheelbarrow. These can be turned into permanent decorative features in the garden or even brought into the house to be shown off.

flowers

A vase of fresh flowers brings immediate
warmth to an interior space filled with
junk objects. Being relatively short-lived,
floral arrangements provide a graceful
counterpoint to the imperfections and
timelessness of old furniture. Choose
plants in vivid shades to introduce an
intense note that will instantly lift the
spirits. Such an injection of vitality will
probably be particularly welcome in
rooms with neutral schemes.

DELICATE TOUCH
this page
*Plain shapes and clear
glass are the best vehicles
for simple flowers.*

FORMAL OR INFORMAL
left, above and below
*A stemmed bowl makes a
perfect table centrepiece,
while a galvanized jug offers
a more casual display.*

INDOOR GARDEN
far left, small pictures
*Mottle-glazed ceramic pots
are ideal for holding all sorts
of floral specimens, short or
tall; or bring terracotta pots in
from the garden and enjoy
the flowers while they bloom.*

**NEW LIFE far left,
above and below**
*An old metal kettle is
now home to a cluster of
cheerful pansies, while
an enamel jug plays host
to hydrangeas.*

**SPIKE
left**
*Plants will be happy in all
manner of containers as
long as they have proper
drainage holes.*

**WELL CONTAINED
right and below right**
*Junk discoveries such
as these buckets make
perfect vases – the
more unexpected the
container the better.*

**PITCHER PERFECT
below**
*Place a few sprays of the
same flower in different
vases close together for
a charming group.*

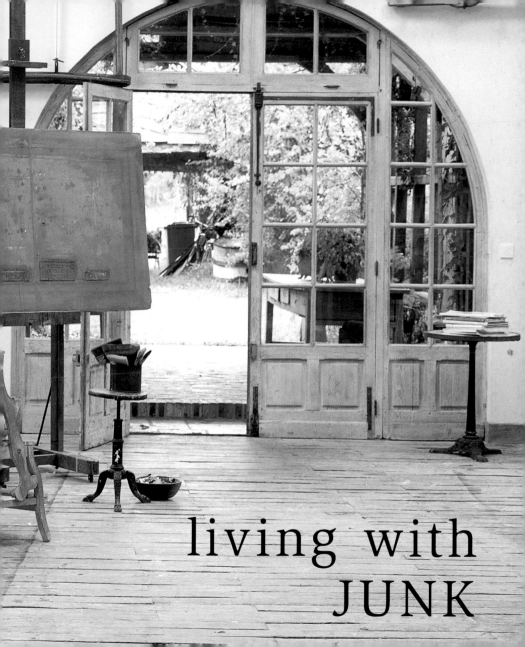

living with
JUNK

living
and dining

Once you have managed to acquire the best second-hand furniture, fabrics and accessories you can find, it is time to put all the elements together to create a home that looks good and is easy to live in. There are no rules about making exact matches, or even about using items for the purpose for which they were designed. One pleasure of using junk is that salvaged pieces bring with them some of the character of their former life – but junk style is not an excuse for wallowing in nostalgia, nor does it seek faithfully to recreate replicas of historical interiors. It is a look that is very much of the moment.

Junk-style interiors are fresh and modern. The less clutter there is, the

CLASSICS left
Twentieth-century,
Le Corbusier-designed
chairs mingle happily
with more humble
flea-market furniture
in a Paris apartment.

BASIC NEEDS above
Decoration is minimal
in this 17th-century grain
store, where no more
than an old picnic basket
and a couple of casual
shirts adorn the walls.

better able we are to appreciate the clean lines of chairs and tables chosen for their strong shapes. Often it will have been a particular colour, shape or texture that attracted you to a second-hand item in the first place – the warm glow of aged wood patinated with the scars of years of use, for example, or the jewel-like shine of coloured glass – so you will want to show off your finds to their best advantage. Spontaneity and a lack of pretension are at the heart of junk style. Whatever pieces

**KEEPING IT SIMPLE
left and this picture**
*A rough garden tool
decorates the wall of Yuri
Kuper's New York loft,*

*while an old pine table
with several mismatched
chairs is well placed to
enjoy the canal view
in Amsterdam.*

you discover will speak for themselves, establishing their own unique style and making everyone who enters your living space feel completely and utterly at home.

For a spacious look with restrained adornment, decorate your living and dining areas with white walls and a few selected treasures. For a busier feel, use rich colours and introduce the paintings and quirky *objets d'art* you have picked up over the years.

If there is space for two or even three sofas, so much the better. Arrange them so that they face one another, perhaps beside a couple of slouchy armchairs, to make a sociable group. Despite the variety of shapes and sizes and the different colours and design of the worn upholstery fabrics, the room will feel harmonious since each of the elements in it is laid-back and unaffected.

If you are lucky enough to have a fireplace, arrange your sofas and chairs in such a way as to make it the room's focus. Look out for old fire-irons, coal scuttles, screens and metal fenders to

set in the hearth. Other junk purchases such as footstools and occasional tables, feather-filled cushions, colourful throws and warm tartan blankets add comfort and convenience. Search for rag mats and woven hearth rugs to give the room yet another layer of softness.

LONG TABLE above
Charlotte Culot bought her generously sized dining table from a flea market in Ardèche.

EATING OUT above right
Minimal restoration was done when this stylish Avignon restaurant, called Woolloomooloo, was converted from an old print works.

RURAL RETREAT right
This reclaimed grain store has been furnished with a charming hotch-potch of finds.

Whether you prefer a separate dining area or tend to eat in the sitting room or kitchen, every home needs a place set aside for enjoying food. Junk style creates a warm and inviting look that is a far cry from the stuffiness of a formal dining room. Here, there is no need to stand on ceremony, because the table is rough-and-ready pine rather than polished mahogany, the candlesticks are hand-blown glass rather than solid silver, and the tablecloth is a simple length of gingham rather than starched white damask.

Table settings can be as plain or as ornate as you like. At one end of the spectrum is a no-frills approach, with a bare wooden table top set with plain white china in a mixture of weights and shapes, old linen napkins, stainless-steel cutlery, chunky tumblers and a jug of flowers. For special occasions, old lace can form the backdrop for floral china, assorted bone-handled silver cutlery, elegant cut-glass goblets and a stemmed crystal dish piled high with fruit as a centrepiece.

ON THE BENCH above
Long benches may have started life as anything from garden furniture to church pews; they are very versatile in dining rooms because they can seat so many people.

WOOD right
The beauty of wooden furniture is that whatever it is made of, from pine to oak, and whatever the finish or colour, it will always look good with other wooden furniture.

kitchens

People tend to gather in the kitchen because it is a place of warmth, somewhere they can go to enjoy good company as well as nourishment, where conversations, meals, work, food preparation and leisure activities can all happily take place alongside one another.

TAKE A SEAT
opposite
*Solid church chairs make
fine kitchen seating.*

KETTLES GALORE
below and left
*Old aluminium items can
be found in abundance.*

Kitchen junk looks at home even in a modern setting. It makes a lovely contrast to stainless-steel cookers and fitted units, and gives authenticity to retro kitchens. You might find yourself choosing fewer pieces than you would for a more country-style kitchen, but the junk elements you do include will really stand out against the room's cool, clean lines.

It can be fun to scour markets and salerooms in search of early examples of kitchen equipment. Pieces dating from decades ago, such as meat mincers, coffee grinders, juicers, nutcrackers and weighing scales with sets of brass or iron weights, were often so well designed and built that they are still going strong today.

As well as being better looking than many of today's plastic or electronic gadgets, yesterday's household goods are also far more satisfying to use. Old utensils have similar aesthetic advantages. Sets of saucepans, tiny metal tea strainers, enamel colanders, ladles, spatulas, rolling pins and sieves

RETRO CHIC left
Designer Roxanne Beis admired the 1940s cupboards she inherited with her Paris flat so much she designed her kitchen around them.

POTS AND PANS above
This matching set of aluminium saucepans with white handles was discovered in a Paris flea market.

can be suspended from a kitchen shelf where they are always close at hand. Keep your eyes open for any other hardware that would introduce extra character to your kitchen, from thermometers, tea trays and caddies to mops, buckets and brooms.

If you want a traditional country kitchen, enhance the reassuringly familiar look by adding an old refectory table, some unpainted wooden cupboards, a few plain rush-seated chairs or long benches and the most basic floor covering you can find; bare boards, terracotta tiles or rush matting are perfect. Keep the look as uncomplicated and utilitarian as possible. Copper pans can be hung up for decoration

BACK TO BASICS
left

This simply furnished wooden barn deep in the Dutch countryside takes guests back to simpler times.

HEART OF THE HOME
right

Painter Charlotte Culot bought her old range from a local village in Provence. The charcoal-burning stove helps to warm the room in winter.

TEA BREAK left

*A portable single gas
burner is just the right
size to hold a kettle of
water for making tea.*

LABELLED UP above
Any lettering on an item, especially if in a foreign language, can add a great deal to its charm.

LIMED WOOD left
The woodwork in this kitchen has been 'aged' with white acrylic paint sanded smooth.

(though any sign of damage means they are not safe actually to cook with), while old stove-top kettles, wooden utensils, salt-glazed storage jars and chunky earthenware pottery can be stowed on open shelves until needed.

Second-hand cooking ranges are always prized for their warmth, good looks and efficiency, but prices tend to reflect the keen demand for machines in sound working condition, so seek the advice of a qualified professional before having one installed to make sure that you are spending your money wisely.

For a slightly more sophisticated kitchen, a different sort of junk sets the tone. Choose an old butler's sink and simple pieces of furniture painted in authentic shades of warm cream, pale blue and soft green. Tongue-and-groove wall panelling looks lovely when given the same treatment. Line shelves with rows of tins and enamelware, or display an assortment of patterned crockery on wall-mounted wooden plate racks or simple cup hooks – all will contribute more to the room's style and mood than their modest price-tag might suggest.

As well as being decorative, old tins can revert to their original purpose and be used to store anything from dried fruit to flour. Other groceries can be stored in old meat safes, wooden crates, baskets, galvanized buckets and even large preserving pans. Cleaning materials can be kept under the sink, concealed by a curtain that has been simply made by gathering a piece of old fabric on a length of wire.

IN THE BALANCE right
Traditional commercial weighing scales have a reliable quality.

LITTLE JUGS below
Jugs are indispensable around the kitchen for serving iced water or holding flowers.

OLD AND NEW
above

A quirky collection of junk containers adds character to a restrained contemporary kitchen.

A UNIFIED WHOLE
right

An accumulation of interesting finds has been put together in this kitchen to create a room full of personality.

GOOD SERVICE
above left and left

The best junk finds earn their keep by being functional as well as looking good.

bedrooms

Your bedroom should be as relaxed and comfortable as any other room in your home – if not more so. Filling a bedroom with junk-shop finds will strike just the right balance between indulgence and simplicity. Imagine a plain wrought-iron bed made up with white cotton sheets and covered with a downy quill, and you willl appreciate the essence of this style.

DISPLAY left
This beautifully battered linen closet was painted to match the monochrome bedroom scheme.

ORNATE IRON this page
The bed came from a flea market in Belgium; its linen was found at Provence's Isle sur la Sorgue market.

FIELD OF DREAMS
above
*Large furniture sales are
the best place to go to
find a range of antique
beds in one place.*

DORMITORY
above right
*These iron beds began
life in a boarding school.
You may find similar
ones in salvage yards –
or check the local press
for announcements of
closing-down sales at
schools or nursing homes.*

Battered antique bedsteads appear in
all the usual junk-lovers' haunts, and
each will create a slightly different mood
and style in a bedroom. Sometimes
headboards are available together with
their bases, mattresses or footboards,
sometimes without. Don't disregard
a beautiful find simply because it is
incomplete, since separate bases and
mattresses can easily be bought or
made to fit. Falling in love with the
headboard itself is the most important
thing. Remember, too, that the most
unusual junk-shop finds can be adapted
to make headboards – gates, plank
doors and carved panels can all be cut

BRASSED OFF left

Examine painted metal bedsteads carefully – you might find brass hidden under the paint.

OLD LINEN below

Simple bed linen with just a hint of decoration is the best dressing for an ornate bed.

GATEWAY
this page

Think beyond the obvious in the bedroom. Weathered wooden gates make quirky head- and footboards.

WELL HANDLED
opposite

Don't be too precious about cleaning up your finds. For example, old handles and flaking paint can add to the charm.

to size and fitted to a base, so keep your mind open to such possibilities while engaged in your search.

Simple metal-framed hospital and dormitory beds are good for children on account of their sturdiness, while more decorative wrought-iron versions, singles or doubles, are ideal for guest rooms. More intricate and flamboyant designs – perhaps a *lit bateau* or a

bed with brass knobs – are probably worth reserving for a master bedroom, where a hint of grandeur can be beautifully offset by the room's more humble elements. A romantic four-poster is a rare junk-shop find, but you could make your own version using reclaimed or recycled timber supports and draping them with white muslin.

The bedroom is a good place to mix old with new: the charm of an old bedstead with the comfort of a modern mattress, or a vintage cotton cover on a new duvet. When buying new pillows, bolsters and quilts, opt for ones that are filled in the traditional manner with duck feathers or, better still, goose down.

Bedroom furniture can be as minimal or as decorative as you like. Near-empty rooms that contain just a bed make a dramatic statement and are somehow deeply appealing. But bear in mind that the peace and tranquillity of this sort of space will quickly be shattered by too much clutter, so avoid this look unless you are impeccably tidy, own very few possessions or have enough space for a separate dressing room. A less austere solution is to add several pieces of junk furniture. Store clothes in a wooden wardrobe, as large as you have space for, a chest of drawers or a linen press – or, alternatively, on a commercial metal clothes rail bought from a wholesale supplier or picked up in a junk sale. When looking for bedside tables, think beyond conventional cabinets and use small round metal café tables, wooden stools or metal seats to allow you to keep your water jug and night-time reading close at hand.

ORIGINAL FEATURES
below

These walls, in a house dating from 1520, have been left virtually as they were discovered after 30 years of neglect.

TRAVELLING BED right

This 1860s travelling bed was found, covered with baggage labels, in a Devon antiques shop.

BATHING IN STYLE
right

This bath travelled on the top of a car from a Brussels flea market to its home in Provençe. An old wooden rack found on a farm has become a quirky towel rail.

SHATTERED GLASS
left

A fragment of mirror perched on the taps is all that's needed.

bathrooms

Serious junk-shoppers find it difficult to resist reclaimed antique bathroom fittings. In comparison with flimsy modern acrylic versions, cast-iron roll-top claw-foot baths are far superior. The same goes for old porcelain sinks set in metal stands, huge chrome daisy-head shower attachments, and Victorian lavatories with their original high-mounted cisterns.

In addition, a few small touches can make all the difference to existing plain white fittings: swap the taps for reconditioned originals, introduce some down-to-earth junk-style accessories, whitewash the walls – and all that remains for you to do is to turn on the taps, lie back and relax.

SAFELY STORED
this page
*Bathrooms are ideal
places for showing off all
those wonderful pieces
of china you've collected.
A classic white jug will
find a home anywhere,
while pretty plates can
hold small items of
bathroom paraphernalia.*

LIGHT AND AIRY
opposite
*A charming basin has
been tucked into the
eaves of this Normandy
barn. The mirror has
been sliced to fit the
space neatly.*

Infinite variety is available to those who are prepared to scour salvage yards and specialist outlets at home and abroad in pursuit of something unique. Stumbling across an old tub used as a cattle trough in the middle of a field is less likely to happen these days – but you may still be lucky. Re-enamelling the bath is always possible if it is otherwise in good shape.

Devotees of junk style do not mind having a sink, bathtub and lavatory that don't match. Nor do they object to using a garden table as a washstand, as long as the spirit of casual simplicity reigns. So combine different styles, designs and functions according to what is available and what looks best.

Once you have established the look of the room with its main fixtures and fittings, try to keep everything else as simple and uncluttered as possible. Bathrooms need a surprising amount of storage space in order to maintain their clean lines. Pieces of furniture imported from elsewhere in the house can all find a home here: store toiletries in a spare

kitchen cupboard, hang bath robes on an unused peg rail brought up from the scullery, or pile towels into an empty blanket box from the bedroom.

Traditional-style items of bathroom furniture are as useful as they ever were, so when you go shopping keep your eyes open for old lockable medicine chests, small mirrored cabinets and old tile-backed washstands. For the sake of

the sink, an old glass tumbler to hold the toothbrushes, a floral-patterned china saucer as a soap dish, or a basic wooden trestle as a towel rail. Similarly, if you can't find a bath mat made in the old-fashioned way from duckboard slats or cork, use a small hearth rug instead.

Flowers give as much pleasure in the bathroom as in any other room, so put a small vase containing a few stems on a bathroom shelf or washstand, or hang up a bunch of lavender to keep the air fresh and sweet-smelling. Together, such small details will enhance the sensual pleasure of your bathroom.

authenticity, combine them with an enamel or porcelain jug and bowl set and piles of soft cotton hand-towels.

Other classic bathroom accessories, such as glass shelf units, mirrors, tooth mugs, toothbrush holders, soap dishes and chunky chrome heated towel rails, also appear from time to time in flea markets. Otherwise, improvise with a piece of driftwood as a bathroom shelf, a gold-framed living-room mirror above

ALL AT SEA
this page
Model ships from a
London warehouse
give this bathroom
a seafaring theme.

NAUTICAL SINK
opposite, left
This buy, from a seaside
junk shop, was once
owned by a sea captain.

SALVAGE JOB
opposite, right
With a little work,
enamelled sinks can be
restored to useful life.

CROSSED WIRES
opposite, above left
Twisted-metalwork containers are ideal for holding bathroom items, since they allow water to drain away.

SOAP STARS
opposite, below left and above right
Enamelware dishes come in all shapes, even shells. Lettering makes them more collectable.

SINKING FEELING
opposite, below left
Keep a lookout for unusually shaped basins – industrial designs are often more interesting than domestic ones.

REINVENTION
this page
This lovely enamel dish, which was formerly an ashtray, is far more suitably employed holding blocks of soap.

TROUGH
right and above

The unusually deep bath in this elegant panelled bathroom is actually a cattle trough that was found abandoned in a Lincolnshire field. The wooden feet were made specially to support it, and the taps have been fitted to the wall to avoid damaging the tub.

SHIP AHOY
far right

White-painted walls and white tiles maximize the light from an old ship's lamp – a characterful accent in a bathroom.

workrooms,
studies and studios

Whether you run a business from home or just need a place to write letters, pay bills, pursue hobbies or store papers, a workspace is essential. Filling your study with modern office furniture would make it efficient, tidy and well-organized, but its dull uniformity and lack of character would leave much to be desired. Turn instead to junk and you can create a space with style, flair and a distinctly human touch. Even in the most minimal environment, a few quirky, characterful pieces will be inspirational. First, choose a location. If you have a whole room at your disposal, it's relatively easy to create a business-like workspace – with the advantage of being able to shut the door on everything at the end of the day. For a less spacious office, but one that can still accommodate a small writing table, use part of a wide landing or the corner of a bedroom or dining room.

First on your shopping list should be a work table. A roll-top desk can be ideal, especially one with lots of built-in drawers,

WORKSTATION
opposite and below
Surround yourself with stylish accessories while you work to create an atmosphere conducive to concentration.

WINDOW SEATS
above and right
Small tables used as impromptu desks make the most of the natural light streaming in through the windows.

letter racks and pen holders. But this sort of piece is not cheap, and a simple kitchen table or console may do just as well. If your studio is used for practical work, such as painting or sewing, a wooden trestle – or even an old door resting on two low cupboards – will more than suffice. A comfortable seat, ideally one that is adjustable and provides good back support, is the next priority. Look for

chairs that were originally intended for use in an office. It seems appropriate to restore such furniture to its primary function; and, by its very nature, good office furniture will have been designed for long-lasting comfort.

Find out when office clearances are taking place in your area, but at the same time keep a look out for older styles at sales and auctions, such as adjustable

architects' chairs with low back supports and wooden swivel chairs on castors – they still look great and their classic clean lines work well in a contemporary, junk-style environment.

You will need to devise ingenious storage solutions to keep documents, stationery, materials, equipment and books under control – especially if space is at a premium. Many people find that they work most productively in uncluttered surroundings. Shelving is essential – whether you use lengths of bare plank and some old bricks or find a cheap bookcase in a junk shop. Office clearances are also an excellent source of pieces such as solid-wood filing cabinets, plain metal drawer units, large plan chests and old metal lockers.

For smaller-scale organization, use an old crystal vase as a pen pot, rattan baskets as in-trays, leather trunks for filing paperwork, and hat boxes for stowing any other odds and ends.

It is hard to disguise the unattractive look of equipment such as fax machines and computers, but an old typewriter or a reconditioned Bakelite telephone will help to redress the balance and prevent high-tech styling from taking over totally.

Adjustable anglepoise desk lamps, also reminiscent of another era, remain practical and stylish options for all kinds of close work.

WORK WITH A VIEW
above

The most basic wooden table can be turned into an inviting desk. Drawers are a useful feature for the storage of small stationery items, while an interesting outlook adds to the appeal.

INSIDE OUT left

*This outbuilding-cum-
garden room is filled with
plants, ladders, trugs and
straw hats in wonderfully
organized chaos.*

conservatories
and greenhouses

A sense of the natural world – with all its wonderful colours
and scents, and all its graceful dust and decay – is what
dictates the atmosphere in a conservatory or a greenhouse.
If you have a space of this kind to call your own, carry an old
wooden bench out there to work on – it can double as a
makeshift dining table in the cooler months of the year when
the garden is out of bounds. Gather old garden tools, either
hanging them from hooks and nails or leaning them up in
a corner ready for use. Apart from the plants, these work-
smoothed trugs, gardening gloves, shears, spades and forks
are the only decoration your conservatory needs.

POTTED HISTORY right

*Timeworn terracotta,
wood, clay and painted
brick give a potting shed
traditional appeal.*

UNDER GLASS far
right, above and below

*A flourishing potting
shed can be a centre
of activity as well as a
place for relaxation.*

LOOKING IN above

Plenty of greenery both inside and out give a subdued and romantic atmosphere to this barn set in an orchard.

BENCH MARK left

Redolont of traditional skills, even the most ordinary workbench can become an understated decorative feature.

OLD WORLD opposite, above and below

A covered studio next to a converted barn is filled with weathered furniture and the artist-owner's own canvasses.

living outdoors

Any patch of garden, however small, can become an outdoor haven in fine weather. Even a narrow balcony or the smallest paved area beside the back door is room enough for a small marble-topped table and white-painted metal chairs where you can eat breakfast or lunch on a summer's day. Furnish it accordingly, treating it with the same care and making use of junk style just as you would inside the home. And just as you can happily use garden furniture indoors, by the same token you can transfer furniture originally designed for the home to an outdoor setting. The visible effects of ageing – such a key part of the appeal of junk style – are accelerated when furniture is directly exposed to the elements. And if you

have picked up an old table and some chairs at little cost, you will not be particularly upset when the paint blisters or lichen makes its home in the cracks of bare wood. Even fabrics can be left to take their chances – for example, deckchair canvas can be allowed to bleach in the sun until its gaudy stripes have faded to shadows. One great pleasure of outdoor living – and one of the most enjoyable

SUMMER LIFE
left
*A semi-covered area
sheltered from the
elements is used as a
seasonal dining room.*

AL FRESCO DELIGHTS
above and far left
*Take lunch or dinner in
the shade of a leafy tree.
Hurricane lamps will give
light as dusk falls.*

GARDEN DISPLAY
above and right
Outdoor ornamentation
takes many forms, from
the pleasingly practical
to the purely decorative.
Visible signs of decay are
an optional extra.

A DOG'S LIFE
above right
Even animals can enjoy
the benefits of junk style.
This contented canine
surveys outdoor activities
from the comfort of a
recycled basket.

TIMEWORN left, below left and above right
Outdoor furniture should not be too delicate – choose pieces with a weathered look to add to the sense of informality.

DAY BED below
Piled with cushions and pillows to soften the hard metal, this ironwork lounger makes a quiet place to relax and enjoy the scenery.

BACK TO NATURE
below right
and opposite
Lunch is served outside
in a part of the orchard
surrounding the house
of artist Yuri Kuper. The
tables and chairs were
designed by Kuper;
their wooden surfaces
have been allowed to
mellow with age and a
covering of lichen.

ABANDONED IN SITU
below
Reminder of a bygone
age, a forgotten plough
lies rusting in a field.

ways of relaxing with friends – is dining outside. Choose a
sheltered position for your garden table and chairs – this
could be on the lawn, in a cobbled clearing at the bottom of
the garden, or closer to the house on a terrace or veranda. So
that you can enjoy al fresco meals in the heat of the midday
sun, ensure that there is some shade – an old parasol, a
canopy of vines or a shady tree will all do the job.

Junk dining furniture made from metal, rattan, wicker or wood
is ideal. If it is slightly faded, rusted or weather-worn to start
with, so much the better. Either leave a wooden table
top on show or throw over a simple checked cloth or an old
white sheet, adding generously filled jugs of garden flowers
to capture the lazy mood of high summer. Add plenty of soft

cushions covered in easy-going cotton if your chairs are not as comfortable as they might be – you could make some oversized covers from an assortment of remnants and keep a spare set to wrap around your living-room cushions.

Set the table with the same pieces you would use for indoor dining. None of your robust glass tumblers, flea-market china plates, worn linen napkins or odd pieces of cutlery is too precious for a trip into the garden, and all are far nicer than the usual plastic knives and forks or paper plates and cups. To allow your guests to enjoy the occasion far into the evening, hang hurricane lamps and storm lanterns in the trees and light them as dusk falls. Cheaper and easier still are old jars with a plain white candle or nightlight inside, protected from any stray breezes.

The relaxed way in which it adapts to life in the garden demonstrates how versatile junk style can be. Who would swap the ease with which possessions can be transferred from house to garden and back again for the tensions and restrictions of conventional living?

SEA VIEW opposite

When you live as close as this to the sea, the beach may become your garden, so use sympathetic materials such as reclaimed wood.

FRESH AIR
left and above

Traditional wooden deck chairs with unbleached canvas seats let visitors enjoy the sea breeze in comfort and style.

sources

COUNTRY AND OUTDOOR FAIRS

Ardingly Antiques Fair (West Sussex) and Newark Antiques Fair (near Nottingham) take place six times a year. Contact DMG Antiques Fairs (01636 702326) www.dmgworldmedia.com

Penman Antiques Fairs are held in Chester, Petersfield and London. Contact Penman Antiques Fairs (01444 482514) www.penman-fairs.co.uk

ANTIQUE MARKETS
Alfie's Antiques Market
13–25 Church Street
London NW8 8DT
020 7723 6066

Bermondsey Antiques Market
158 Bermondsey Street
London SE1
(Friday 5a.m.–2p.m.)

Brick Lane Market
Brick Lane, London E1
(Sunday morning)

The Furniture Cave
533 Kings Road
London SW10 0TZ
020 7352 4229

Grays Antique Market
58 Davies Street
London W1 1AR
020 7629 7034

The Mall Antiques Arcade
Camden Passage
359 Upper Street
London N1 0PD
Portobello Road Market
London W11 (Saturday)

SALVAGE
www.architectural-salvage.co.uk

www.baileys-home-garden.co.uk
01989 561931

Dorset Reclamation
Cow Drove, Bere Regis
Dorset BH20 7JZ
01929 472200

The House Hospital
9 Ferrier Street
London SW18 1SW
020 8870 8202

LASSCo
St Michael's Church
Mark Street
London EC2A 4ER
020 7749 9944
www.lassco.co.uk/antiques

Peco
72 Station Road
Hampton
Middlesex TW12 2AX
020 8979 8310

Walcot Reclamation
108 Walcot Street
Bath
Somerset BA1 5BG
01225 444404
www.walcot.com

Wells Reclamation
Coxley Wells
Somerset BA5 1RQ
01749 677087

AUCTION HOUSES
Lots Road Auctions
71–73 Lots Road
London SW10 0RN
020 7376 6800
www.lotsroad.com

General Auction
63–65 Garratt Lane
London SW18 4AA
020 8870 3909

Parkins
18 Malden Road
Cheam
Surrey SM3 8QF
020 8644 6633

FURNITURE AND ACCESSORIES
After Noah
121 Upper Street
London N1 1QP
020 7359 4281
www.afternoah.com

Antiques and Things
91 Eccles Road
London SW11 1LX
020 7350 0597

Appley Hoare
30 Pimlico Road
London SW1W 8LJ
020 7730 7070

Bazar
82 Golborne Road
London W10 5PS
020 8969 6262

Bed Bazaar
The Old Railway Station
Station Road
Framlingham
Suffolk IP13 9EE
01728 723756

Brass Knight Brass Bedsteads
Cumeragh Lane
Whittingham
Preston
Lancashire PR3 2AL
01772 786666

Cath Kidston
8 Clarendon Cross
London W11 4AP
020 7221 4000
www.cathkidston.co.uk

Decorative Living
55 New King's Road
London SW6 4SE
020 7736 5623

Eccles Road Antiques
60 Eccles Road
London SW11 1LX
020 7228 1638

Josephine Ryan Antiques
63 Abbeville Road
London SW4 9JW
020 8675 3900

Judy Greenwood Antiques
657 Fulham Road
London SW6 5PY
020 7736 6037

The Lacquer Chest
75 Kensington Church Street
London W8 4BG
020 7937 1306

MAC Architectural & Decorative Antiques
86 Golborne Road
London W10 5PS
020 8960 3736

Manor Farm Antiques
159 Abingdon Road
Standlake
Witney
Oxfordshire OX29 7RL
01865 300303

Mark Maynard Antiques
651 Fulham Road
London SW6 5PU
020 7731 3533

Myriad Antiques
131 Portland Road
London W11 4LW
020 7229 1709

Nimmo & Spooner Antiques
277 Lillie Road
London SW6 7LL
020 7385 2724

Pimpernel & Partners
596 Kings Road
London SW6 2EL
020 7731 2448

Stiffkey Bathrooms
89 Upper St Giles Street
Norwich
Norfolk NR2 1AB
01603 627850
www.stiffkey
bathrooms.com

Tobias and The Angel
68 White Hart Lane
London SW13 0PZ
020 8296 0058

KITCHENS
Fens
46 Lots Road
London SW10 0QF
020 7352 9883

Flying Duck
320–22 Creek Road
London SE10 9SW
020 8858 1964

Magpies
152 Wandsworth Bridge
Road
London SW6 2UH
020 7736 3738

Summerill & Bishop
100 Portland Road
London W11 4LQ
020 7221 4500

**OFFICE AND
INDUSTRIAL**
Castle Gibson
106a Upper Street
London N1 1QN
020 7704 0927

**Key Industrial
Equipment**
Blackmoor Road
Ebblake Industrial Estate
Verwood
Dorset BH31 6AT
0800 5870623
www.keyind.co.uk

FABRICS
The Curtain Agency
231 London Road
Camberley
Surrey GU15 3EY
01276 671672

Lunn Antiques
86 New King's Road
London SW6 4LU
020 7736 4638

Pavilion Antiques
Freshford Hall
Freshford, Bath
Somerset BA3 6EJ
(by appointment only)
01225 722522

**OUTDOOR AND
GARDEN**
**Arne Maynard
Garden Design**
125 Golden Lane
London EC1Y 0TJ
020 7689 8100

Clifton Nurseries
5a Clifton Villas
London W9 2PH
020 7289 6851

**Heritage Oak
Buildings**
Benefold Farm
Petworth
West Sussex GU28 9NX
01798 344066

Peter Hone
5 Ladbroke Square
London W11 3LX
(garden antiques
consultant;
by appointment only)

**SPECIALIST
SUPPLIERS**
Alexis Aufray
Artelano
54 Rue de Bourgogne
75007 Paris
France
(lighting design)
+ 33 1 44 18 00 00
www.artelano.com

Havenplan
The Old Station
Station Road
Killamarsh
Sheffield
South Yorkshire S21 1EN
(period doors)
0114 2489972

Looking For Ages
East Hill
Parracombe
Devon EX31 4PF
(traditional door furniture)
01598 763300

**Prices Patent
Candles**
100 York Road
London SW11 3RD
020 7924 6336

**FOREIGN SOURCES:
MARKETS**
L'Isle sur la Sorgue
France (April and August)

**Marché aux Puces de
St Ouen**
Rue de Rosiers
St Ouen, Paris
France

Noordermarkt
Noorderstraat
Amsterdam
The Netherlands
(Monday 9 a.m. 2 p.m.)

Puce de Vanves
Avenues de la Porte de
Vanves and George
Lafenestre/Rue Marc
Sangnier
Paris
France
(Saturday/Sunday
7 a.m.–1 p.m.)

St Jansvliet
Antwerp
Belgium
(Sunday 9 a.m.-5 p.m.)

**FOREIGN SOURCES:
SHOPS**
280 Modern
280 Lafayette Street
New York, NY 10012
USA
+ 1 212 941 5825

Anthropologie
375 West Broadway
New York, NY 10012
USA
+ 1 212 343 7070
www.anthropologie.com

Coming to America
276 Lafayette Street
New York, NY 10012
USA
+ 1 212 343 2968

Fishs Eddy
889 Broadway
New York, NY 10003
USA
+ 1 212 420 2090
www.fishseddy.com

Potted Gardens
41 King Street
New York, NY 10014
USA
+ 1 212 255 4797
www.colecreates.com

Ruby Beets Antiques
1703 Montauk Highway
Bridgehampton
NY 11932
USA
+ 1 516 537 2802

**Xavier Nicod and
Gérard Nicod**
9 Avenue des Quatre
Otages
848000 L'Isle sur
la Sorgue
France
+ 33 4 90 38 07 20

index

acknowledgments

My thanks go to Tom Leighton, for his kindness and good humour and for always taking beautiful pictures whatever the weather, and to Simon Whitmore, his assistant, for keeping us on the right road. Also to Larraine Shamwana, for her consistent encouragement and great art direction – her huge contribution to pulling this project together creatively will not be forgotten. I couldn't have asked for a better team to travel and work with.

Junk Style would not have come together at all without the wonderful houses we were allowed to photograph, so I am indebted to their owners, all of whom seemed to share the same spirit and made the photography for this book so memorable: garden antiques expert Peter Hone, garden designer Arne Maynard, Marilyn Phipps, interior designer Philip Hooper, artist Yuri Kuper, painter Charlotte Culot and lighting designer Alexis Aufray, designers Roxanne Beis and Jean-Bernard Navier, Netty Nauta, Caroline and Michael Breet, Aleid Rontgen and Annette Brederode, Glen Senk and Keith Johnson of Anthropologie, Jim and Pat Cole of Coming to America, and George Laaland at Woolloomooloo Restaurant. I am grateful to the following shops for kindly allowing us to photograph their collections of second-hand furniture and accessories: Xavier Nicod, Potted Gardens, Ruby Beets and Fishs Eddy. I would also like to thank all my friends and colleagues who helped me to locate the shops, especially Polly and Mark Gilbey in London, Roxanne Beis and Amelie Thiodet in France, Nina Monfils in Holland and Andrea Raisfeld in New York.

Thanks to my sister Caroline for her translations, to Fiona Craig McFeely and Jo Tyler for their help, to my agent Fiona Lindsay and all at Ryland Peters & Small. Thanks also to my brilliant sons, George and Ralph, for taking my frequent absences in good humour, and to Belinda for keeping things together at home. Above all, thanks to my wonderful husband, Martin, for everything.